W9-ASL-437

GRASSLAND
FOOD WEBS

BY PAUL FLEISHER

LERNER PUBLICATIONS COMPANY • MINNEAPOLIS

The photographs in this book are used with the permission of: © Bill Allen, backgrounds on pp. 1, 6, 14, 22, 27, 34, 39, 44–45, 46–47; © Greg Neise/Visuals Unlimited, p. 5; © Richard Thom/Visuals Unlimited, pp. 6, 43; © Adam Jones/Visuals Unlimited, p. 7; © Wally Eberhart/Visuals Unlimited, p. 8; © Steve Maslowski/Visuals Unlimited, pp. 9, 35, 48 (top); © S. Purdy Matthews/Stone/Getty Images, p. 10; © John and Barbara Gerlach/Visuals Unlimited, p. 11; © Leonard Lee Rue III/Photo Researchers, Inc., p. 12; © Arthur Morris/Visuals Unlimited, p. 13; © Stacy D. Gold/National Geographic/Getty Images, p. 14; © Martin Harvey/Gallo Images/Getty Images, p. 16; © Inga Spence/Visuals Unlimited, pp. 17, 39; © David Muench/CORBIS, p. 18; © Scientifica/Visuals Unlimited, p. 19; © Joel Sartore/National Geographic/Getty Images, p. 20; © Annie Griffiths Belt/National Geographic/Getty Images, p. 21; © David Madison/The Image Bank/Getty Images, p. 22; © Raymond Coleman/Visuals Unlimited, p. 23; © W. Wayne Lockwood, M.D./CORBIS, p. 24; © Gunter Marx Photography/CORBIS, p. 25; © Gerald & Buff Corsi/Visuals Unlimited, p. 26; National Park Service Photo by Roy Wood, p. 27; National Park Service Photo by RG Johnsson, p. 28; © W. Perry Conway/CORBIS, p. 29; © Joe McDonald/Visuals Unlimited, pp. 30, 34; © Michael & Patricia Fogden/Minden Pictures/Getty Images, p. 31; © Steve Kaufman/CORBIS, p. 32; National Park Service Photo by J. Schmidt, p. 33; © Dr. Dennis Kunkel/Visuals Unlimited, p. 36; © Gary Braasch/CORBIS, p. 37; © Dr. James L. Castner/Visuals Unlimited, p. 38; © Dorling Kindersley/Getty Images, p. 40; © Harrison Shull/Aurora/Getty Images, p. 41; © Colin Monteath/Hedgehog House/Minden Pictures/Getty Images, p. 42; © Tom Bean/Photographer's Choice/Getty Images, p. 46; © Eric and David Hoskins/CORBIS, p. 47; © Tom Bean/CORBIS, p. 48 (bottom). Illustrations on pp. 4, 15 by Zeke Smith, © Lerner Publishing Group, Inc.

Front Cover: U.S. Fish and Wildlife Service (left and middle); PhotoDisc Royalty Free by Getty Images (right); © Bill Allen (background).

Lerner Publications Company
A division of Lerner Publishing Group, Inc.
241 First Avenue North
Minneapolis, MN 55401 U.S.A

Website address: www.lernerbooks.com

Library of Congress Cataloging-in-Publication Data

Fleisher, Paul.
    Grassland food webs / by Paul Fleisher.
      p.   cm. — (Early bird food webs)
    Includes index.
    ISBN 978–0–8225–6730–1 (lib. bdg. : alk. paper)
    1. Grassland ecology—Juvenile literature. 2. Food chains (Ecology)—Juvenile literature. I. Title.
QH541.5.P7F58 2008
577.4—dc22   2007001374

Manufactured in the United States of America
1 2 3 4 5 6 – JR – 13 12 11 10 09 08

CONTENTS

A Grassland Food Web

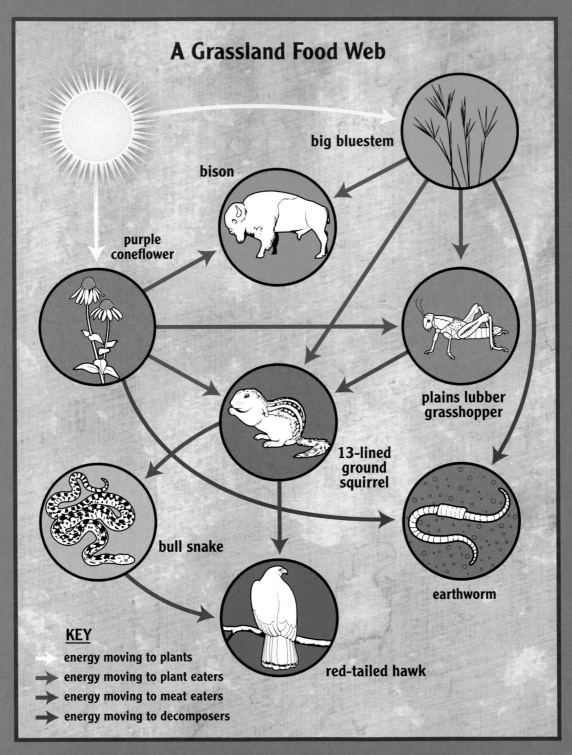

big bluestem

bison

purple coneflower

plains lubber grasshopper

13-lined ground squirrel

bull snake

earthworm

red-tailed hawk

KEY
→ energy moving to plants
→ energy moving to plant eaters
→ energy moving to meat eaters
→ energy moving to decomposers

BE A WORD DETECTIVE

Can you find these words as you read about grassland food webs? Be a detective and try to figure out what they mean. You can turn to the glossary on page 46 for help.

bacteria	environments	omnivores
carnivores	food chain	oxygen
consumers	food web	photosynthesis
decay	herbivores	prairies
decomposers	nutrients	producers

This place is a grassland.
Where are grasslands found?

CHAPTER 1
GRASSLANDS

Tall grasses bend in the wind. Insects buzz in
the warm air. Birds soar through the clear, blue
sky. There are few trees. You can see for miles.
You are in a grassland.

Grasslands are found in many parts of the world. In the United States and Canada, grasslands are called prairies. In other places, they are called pampas, steppes, or savannas.

Grasslands are found in places that don't get enough rain for many large trees to grow. Instead, grasses and other low plants grow there. These plants need less water than big trees.

In Africa, grasslands are called savannas. Savannas have only a few trees.

Grasslands are some of Earth's most important environments. An environment is the place where any creature lives. The environment includes the air, soil, weather, and other plants and animals.

Pronghorn antelopes eat grasses and other plants.

Foxes eat meat. This fox is eating a duck.

Plants and animals in a grassland depend on one another. Some animals eat plants. Some animals are meat eaters. They eat other animals. When plants and animals die, they break down into chemicals (KEH-muh-kuhlz). The chemicals become part of the soil. Some of these chemicals help plants grow.

Energy moves from one living thing to another. A food chain shows how the energy moves. The energy for life comes from the sun. Plants store the sun's energy in their leaves, stems, and roots. When an animal eats a plant, the animal gets some of the sun's energy from the plant. The energy moves farther along the food chain each time one living thing eats another.

A lion is hunting a zebra. If the lion eats the zebra, the lion will get energy from the zebra.

This prairie dog is eating grass.

Grasslands have many food chains. Imagine that a prairie dog eats some grass. Then a hawk eats the prairie dog. When the hawk dies, a vulture eats its body. The sun's energy passes from the grass to the prairie dog. Then it goes to the hawk. Then it passes to the vulture.

This red-tailed hawk is eating a rattlesnake.

But prairie dogs don't eat only grass. They eat many different kinds of plants. Hawks eat other animals besides prairie dogs. They also eat mice and small birds. And vultures eat all kinds of dead animals. An environment's food web is made of many food chains. A food web shows how all creatures depend on one another for food.

This turkey vulture is eating a dead raccoon.

A grassland's energy comes from the sun. Plants use sunlight to make food. What else do plants make?

CHAPTER 2

GRASSLAND PLANTS

Plants use sunlight to make food. Because plants produce food, they are called producers. Plants also make oxygen (AHK-sih-juhn). Oxygen is a gas in the air. All animals need oxygen to breathe.

The way plants make food and oxygen is called photosynthesis (FOH-toh-SIHN-thuh-sihs). Plants need carbon dioxide, sunlight, and water for photosynthesis. Carbon dioxide is a gas in the air. A plant's leaves take in carbon dioxide and sunlight. The plant's roots take in water. The plant uses energy from sunlight to turn the carbon dioxide and water into sugar and starch. Sugar and starch are the plant's own food. The plant stores this food in its leaves and roots.

Photosynthesis

sunlight

carbon dioxide

oxygen

Big bluestem grass's leaves turn sunlight, carbon dioxide and water into food for the plant.

water (from roots)

As the plant makes food, it also makes oxygen. The oxygen goes into the air. Animals breathe in the oxygen. They breathe out carbon dioxide. Plants use the carbon dioxide to make more food.

All animals breathe oxygen. These animals are guanacos. They live in grasslands in South America.

Soil has nutrients that plants need to grow.

Plants grow in soil. The soil contains special chemicals called nutrients (NOO-tree-uhnts). Living things need nutrients to grow. When it rains, water soaks into the soil. Nutrients from the soil go into the water. When a plant's roots take in the water, the plant gets nutrients from the soil too. The nutrients become part of the plant.

Grasses are the most important plants in a grassland. Many different grasses grow on the prairie. Big bluestem, Indian grass, and switchgrass are prairie grasses.

Some prairie grasses grow up to 9 feet tall. That's taller than a basketball player!

Grass plants have long roots. The roots are usually longer than the plant is tall.

Prairie grasses have long roots. The roots grow deep into the ground. The roots hold the soil in place. They keep the soil from being blown away or washed away by rain.

When the prairie gets very dry, the leaves of the grasses die. But under the ground, the roots stay alive. When it rains, new leaves grow from the roots.

Other plants grow on prairies too. Wildflowers grow among the grasses. Sunflowers, coneflowers, clover, and daisies grow there.

The prairie has some bushes and small trees too. Chokecherry, wild plum, crabapple, and prairie rose grow on the prairie. Sagebrush grows in drier parts of the prairie.

Many different kinds of wildflowers grow on the prairie.

Cottonwood trees are growing along the banks of this river.

A few larger trees grow on the prairie.
They grow near streams or ponds. In these
places, trees can get enough water to grow.
Cottonwood, walnut, hackberry, and maple trees
grow on the prairie.

Zebras and gazelles are plant eaters that live in Africa. What are some other animals that eat plants?

CHAPTER 3
GRASSLAND PLANT EATERS

Animals are called consumers. *Consume* means "eat." Animals that eat plants are called herbivores (ER-buh-vorz). The sun's energy is stored inside plants. When an animal eats a plant, it gets the sun's energy.

Many insects are herbivores. Caterpillars, grasshoppers, and leafhoppers eat grasses and other plants. Butterflies, moths, and bees drink nectar. Nectar is a sweet liquid flowers make.

Grasshoppers eat grasses and other kinds of plants.

Many grassland birds eat plant seeds. Goldfinches crack seeds in their beaks. Sparrows and pheasants (FEHZ-uhnts) eat seeds too.

Pheasants eat plant seeds, berries, and insects.

Pocket gophers live in holes in the ground. They eat plant roots, grasses, and seeds.

Prairie dogs, rabbits, and pocket gophers are also herbivores. They live in holes in the ground. Living underground helps these animals stay safe. When they are underground, it is harder for meat eaters to find and eat them.

Bison live on the prairie too. They move from place to place, eating prairie grasses. Pronghorn antelopes also eat prairie grasses.

Long ago, huge herds of bison lived on the prairie.

Prairie rattlesnakes eat meat. What do we call animals that eat meat?

CHAPTER 4
GRASSLAND MEAT EATERS

Some grassland animals eat meat. These animals are called carnivores (KAHR-nuh-vorz). Carnivores eat animals. But they need plants too. Carnivores get energy by eating animals that have eaten plants.

Spiders are carnivores. Some spiders weave sticky webs. They use the webs to catch insects to eat. Wasps hunt insects too. They feed the insects to their babies.

A crab spider is sitting on this sunflower. If an insect visits the flower, the spider will try to catch it.

A cowbird is sitting on this bison's back.

Many birds eat insects. Cowbirds follow big animals such as bison. When bison walk, they scare insects. The insects fly away from the bison. Then cowbirds catch the insects. Bluebirds and red-winged blackbirds eat insects too.

Other kinds of birds are also carnivores.
Kestrels eat small birds. Red-tailed hawks fly
high above the prairie. They hunt birds,
snakes, and lizards.

Kestrels are sometimes called sparrow hawks because they eat small birds. Kestrels also eat insects, mice, lizards, and other small animals.

This milk snake is eating a rat.

Milk snakes eat small animals. They hunt mice, pocket gophers, lizards, other snakes, and birds. They also eat bird eggs.

Foxes are carnivores. They hunt mice, rabbits, pocket gophers, and prairie dogs. They eat birds and snakes too.

Weasels and ferrets are long and thin. They can crawl into the underground holes where small animals live. Weasels and ferrets hunt prairie dogs, gophers, mice, and rats.

Ferrets have long, narrow bodies.

This coyote is hunting for mice.

Some animals eat both plants and meat. These animals are called omnivores (AHM-nuh-vorz). Box turtles are omnivores. They eat leaves, fruit, snails, worms, insects, and bird eggs. Coyotes (kye-OHT-eez) are omnivores too. Coyotes hunt small animals. They also eat bird eggs and fruit.

These are the bones of a deer. The rest of the deer's body has been eaten away. What do we call living things that feed on dead animals?

CHAPTER 5

GRASSLAND DECOMPOSERS

All living things die. When plants and animals die, they decay. They break down into nutrients. Living things called decomposers help dead things decay. Decomposers feed on dead plants and animals.

Decomposers are nature's recyclers. They break down dead plants and animals. Nutrients from the dead plants and animals go into the soil. Then other living things can use the nutrients.

Decomposers are very important. Without them, grasslands would be full of dead plants and animals. Then no new plants could grow. Animals would run out of food.

Earthworms eat dead plants. They break the plants down into nutrients.

The prairie's most important decomposers live in the soil. Bacteria are tiny living things. They are much too small to see. Millions of them live in soil. Mushrooms and other fungi (FUN-jye) live in the soil too. Bacteria and fungi feed on dead plants and animals.

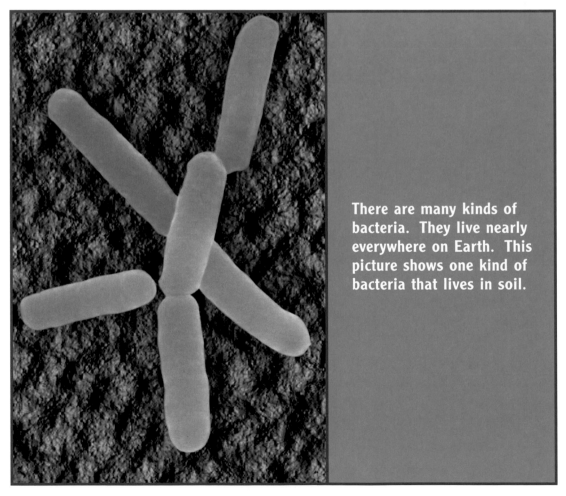

There are many kinds of bacteria. They live nearly everywhere on Earth. This picture shows one kind of bacteria that lives in soil.

Young beetles ate holes in this piece of rotting wood.

Earthworms burrow in the soil. They eat bits of dead leaves. Some insects lay eggs in rotting wood. Young insects hatch from the eggs. The young insects eat the wood.

When an animal dies, insects lay their eggs in its body. The young insects feed on the animal's body. Vultures and box turtles also eat animals that have died.

Maggots are young flies. Maggots feed on the bodies of dead animals.

These cattle are eating grass. Why do people raise cattle?

CHAPTER 6
PEOPLE AND GRASSLANDS

Grasslands are important to people. Many people live on the prairie. They live in towns and cities.

The prairie is a good place for cattle to live. The cattle eat prairie grasses. People raise cattle to get beef to eat. Beef is meat that comes from cattle.

This farmer is plowing the ground to plant crops.

Prairie soil is good for growing crops. Farmers grow wheat and corn on the prairie. People need these crops for food. Usually farmers plow the ground before they plant crops. Plowing breaks up the soil so crops can be planted in rows.

But plowing can harm grasslands. Plowing cuts the roots of prairie plants. The roots no longer hold the soil in place. Wind can blow the soil away. Rain can wash it away. Without soil, plants can't grow.

Farmers can plant some crops without plowing. That way, the roots of dead plants stay in the ground. They hold the soil in place. Planting trees along the edges of fields protects the soil too. The trees block some of the wind. That helps keep the soil from blowing away.

Trees are growing around these farm fields. The trees help to keep the soil from blowing away.

People need water to drink, wash, and grow crops. But people who live on the prairie must not use too much water. If people waste water, streams may dry up. Then prairie plants and animals might not have enough water.

Some plants and animals can live only in grasslands. If people turn all of the prairie into cities and farms, those plants and animals will lose their homes. They will disappear forever.

Grassland animals and plants need water to live.

Osage Prairie is a grassland park in the state of Missouri.

People can protect some grasslands by making them into parks. In these parks, no one plows the ground. No one mows the grasses. Wild plants and animals can live in the parks. Prairie grasses can grow deep roots.

Some places in the United States have prairie parks. Other parts of the world have grassland parks too. It's important to save these grasslands as they were long ago.

ON SHARING A BOOK

When you share a book with a child, you show that reading is important. To get the most out of the experience, read in a comfortable, quiet place. Turn off the television and limit other distractions, such as telephone calls. Be prepared to start slowly. Take turns reading parts of this book. Stop occasionally and discuss what you're reading. Talk about the photographs. If the child begins to lose interest, stop reading. When you pick up the book again, revisit the parts you have already read.

BE A VOCABULARY DETECTIVE

The word list on page 5 contains words that are important in understanding the topic of this book. Be word detectives and search for the words as you read the book together. Talk about what the words mean and how they are used in the sentence. Do any of these words have more than one meaning? You will find the words defined in a glossary on page 46.

WHAT ABOUT QUESTIONS?

Use questions to make sure the child understands the information in this book. Here are some suggestions:

> What did this paragraph tell us? What does this picture show? What is a food web? How do plants depend on animals? Where does a grassland's energy come from? What do we call animals that eat both plants and animals? How does plowing hurt the prairie? What is your favorite part of the book? Why?

If the child has questions, don't hesitate to respond with questions of your own, such as What do *you* think? Why? What is it that you don't know? If the child can't remember certain facts, turn to the index.

INTRODUCING THE INDEX

The index helps readers find information without searching through the whole book. Turn to the index on page 48. Choose an entry such as *plants* and ask the child to use the index to find out how plants make their own food. Repeat with as many entries as you like. Ask the child to point out the differences between an index and a glossary. (The index helps readers find information, while the glossary tells readers what words mean.)

GRASSLANDS AND FOOD WEBS

BOOKS
Capeci, Anne. *Food Chain Frenzy*. New York: Scholastic, 2003.

Dvorak, David, Jr. *A Sea of Grass: The Tallgrass Prairie*. New York: Macmillan, 1994.

Johnson, Rebecca L. *A Walk in the Prairie*. Minneapolis: Lerner Publications Company, 2001.

Landau, Elaine. *Grassland Mammals*. New York: Children's Press, 1996.

Patent, Dorothy Hinshaw. *Prairies*. New York: Holiday House, 1996.

Riley, Peter. *Food Chains*. New York: Franklin Watts, 1998.

MacAulay, Kelley, and Bobbie Kalman. *Prairie Food Chains*. New York: Crabtree Publishing Co., 2005.

WEBSITES
Biomes of the World: Grasslands
http://www.mbgnet.net/sets/grasslnd
This website includes photos of many plants and animals that live in grasslands around the world.

Chain Reaction
http://www.ecokids.ca/pub/eco_info/topics/frogs/chain_reaction
Create a food chain and find out what happens if one link is taken out of the chain.

Food Chains and Webs
http://www.vtaide.com/png/foodchains.htm
This website has an interactive tool to let you create your own food webs.

Grassland Animal Printouts
http://www.enchantedlearning.com/biomes/grassland/grassland.shtml
This page has links to information about many kinds of animals that live in grasslands around the world.

GLOSSARY

bacteria: tiny living things that are made up of just one cell. Bacteria can be seen only under a microscope.

carnivores (KAHR-nuh-vorz): animals that eat meat

consumers: living things that eat other living things. Animals are consumers.

decay: to break down

decomposers: living things that feed on dead plants and animals

environments: places where creatures live. An environment includes the air, soil, weather, plants, and animals in a place.

food chain: the way energy moves from the sun to a plant, then to a plant eater, then to a meat eater, and finally to a decomposer

food web: many food chains connected together. A food web shows how all living things in a place need one another for food

herbivores (ER-buh-vorz): animals that eat only plants

nutrients (NOO-tree-uhnts): chemicals that living things need in order to grow

omnivores (AHM-nuh-vorz): animals that eat both plants and meat

oxygen (AHK-sih-juhn): a gas in the air. All animals need oxygen to breathe.

photosynthesis (FOH-toh-SIHN-thuh-sihs): the way green plants use energy from sunlight to make their own food out of carbon dioxide and water

prairies: grasslands in the United States and Canada

producers: living things that make their own food. Plants are producers.

INDEX

Pages listed in **bold** type refer to photographs.

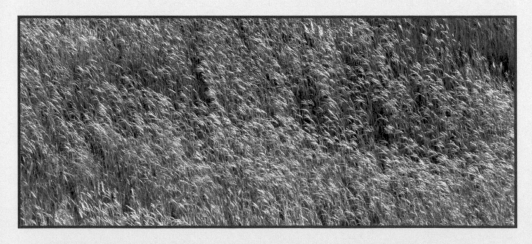